KU-132-461

HEALTHY BODY

Drink and Drugs and Your Body

Polly Goodman

HODDER
Wayland

an imprint of Hodder Children's Books

HEALTHY BODY

This book is based on the original title *How Do Drink and Drugs Affect Me?* by Emma Haughton, in the *Health and Fitness* series, published in 1999 by Hodder Wayland

This differentiated text edition is written by Polly Goodman and published in Great Britain in 2005 by Hodder Wayland, an imprint of Hodder Children's Books.

Editor: Kirsty Hamilton
Designer: Jane Hawkins
Consultant: Jayne Wright

Picture acknowledgments:
Digital Vision 42; Image Bank 4 (Rod Westwood), 10, 11 (David de Lossy), 20 (Gabriel Covian), 22 (Bokelberg), 24 (Nicholas Russell), 28, 31 top (Color Day), 32 (Steve McAlister), 40 (Barros & Barros); Science Photo Library 16 (Dr E Walker), 18 (Damien Lovegrove), 25 bottom (A. Glauberman), 29 (Jim Selby), 35 (Wesley Bocxe), 37 (Cordelia Molloy), 38 (BSIP Laurent), 39 (Tek Image), 41 (Cordelia Molloy), 43 (Will & Deni McIntyre); Stock Market 1, 5 (Robert Cerri), 9, 13, 19, 23, 26, 27 (Roy McMahon), 45; Tony Stone Images 6 (David Harry Stewart), 7 (Steve Taylor), 8 (Jean-Marc Truchet), 12 (Peter Dokus), 14 (Chad Slattery), 17 (Douet/TSI Imaging), 21 (Tim Hazael), 31 bottom (Simon Norfolk), 33 (Demetrio Carrasco), 34 (David Young Wolff), 36 (Zigy Kaluzny), 44 (Mark Harwood); The artwork on pages 15 and 25 is by Michael Posen.

All possible care has been taken to trace the ownership of each photograph and to obtain permission for its use. If there are any omissions or if any errors have occurred, they will be corrected in subsequent editions, on notification to the publisher.

British Library Cataloguing in Publication Data
Goodman, Polly
Drink and drugs and your body. - Differentiated ed. -
(Healthy Body)
1. Alcohol - Physiological effect - Juvenile literature
2. Drugs - Physiological effect - Juvenile literature
3. Substance abuse - Juvenile literature
I. Title
613.8

ISBN 0 7502 47169

Printed in China

Hodder Children's Books
A division of Hodder Headline Limited
338 Euston Road, London NW1 3BH

Contents

What are Drugs?

Drugs change the way the body works. They make people feel different. Some drugs come from plants, animals or minerals. Others are made artificially.

People have been using drugs for thousands of years. American Indians made a stimulant from a type of cactus over 10,000 years ago. The Chinese have used herbal medicines for over 5,000 years.

◀ Coffee and cigarettes contain two of the most common drugs taken for pleasure – caffeine and nicotine.

Taking Drugs

Drugs can be taken in different ways. They can be swallowed through the mouth, inhaled through the lungs, injected directly into the blood, or absorbed through the skin.

Different uses

There are many different kinds of drugs and they are used for different things. Some, such as aspirin, paracetamol and antibiotics are used as medicines. Others, such as caffeine, which is found in tea, coffee and chocolate, are used for pleasure. They are called recreational drugs.

Scientists are working on new drugs every day to treat serious diseases like cancer. Some are made from chemicals in a laboratory, but others come from newly discovered plants. Many of these precious plants are found in the Amazon and other rainforests of the world, which makes it essential to protect these habitats.

Cola contains the drug caffeine, which is also found in coffee and tea. ▶

Where do they come from?

NAME	USED FOR	WHERE DOES IT COME FROM?
Aspirin	Painkiller	Bark of the willow tree
Caffeine	Stimulant	Coffee beans, cocoa and tea leaves
Cannabis	Recreation	Cannabis plant
Digitalis	Heart	Foxgloves
Taxol	Cancer	Yew trees
Tobacco	Recreation	Tobacco plant

Illegal drugs

Many countries have banned the use of certain drugs because they can be dangerous. Heroin, cocaine, speed, ecstasy and cannabis are all illegal to sell or buy in most countries. In Saudi Arabia and some other Muslim countries, alcohol is illegal because it is banned by Islamic law. But some of these drugs were not always banned. Cocaine used to be an ingredient in the drink cola until doctors discovered that it was addictive.

All drugs, even legal ones, are dangerous if they are taken in large quantities. Too much alcohol or tobacco can shorten a person's life. Too much alcohol can endanger other people's lives if they are hit by someone who drinks and drives.

Alcohol doesn't look like a dangerous drug, but it can become addictive. ▼

Legal in Britain?

DRUG	LEGAL?	CONDITIONS
Alcohol	Yes	Not for children under 18 in public
Amphetamines (speed)	Yes	Only on prescription
Cannabis	No	
Cocaine	No	
Ecstasy	No	
Hallucinogenic drugs	No	
Heroin	Yes	Only on prescription
Sleeping tablets	Yes	Only on prescription
Tobacco	Yes	Illegal to sell to children
Tranquillizers	Yes	Only on prescription

Some people believe that since alcohol is just as dangerous as cannabis, both drugs should be treated the same by law so both should be legal.

The leaves of the cannabis plant have been smoked or chewed on for centuries. ▶

Cannabis

Cannabis can relieve the pain of arthritis and cancer sufferers, so some people argue it should be made a legal medicine.

Alcohol

Alcohol is a chemical made from fermented sugars. The sugars come from grain, grapes or other fruits. When they are fermented, they are used to make wine, beer and spirits. When it is drunk, alcohol is absorbed into the bloodstream, where it can have a powerful effect on the body and mind.

The Romans first made wine from grapes over 2,000 years ago. In Northern Europe, beer has been brewed from grain and hops for hundreds of years.

▲ The French are famous for their wines.

Today there are many different types of wine, beer and spirits. Wines range from fizzy champagnes to deep reds. Beers are made into pale lagers or dark bitters. Spirits can be flavoured and sweetened to make liqueurs, or they can be mixed with traditional soft drinks like lemonade to make alcopops.

Alcoholic Strength

The amount of alcohol in a drink is known as its proof. It is often marked on the sides of bottles or cans as a percentage. The higher the percentage, the less you can drink before the alcohol affects you.

Different attitudes

Alcohol is a recreational drug, but different cultures have different attitudes towards it. In France, having fine wines has been a sign of good taste for hundreds of years. In some countries alcohol is not permitted for religious reasons. In America, Canada, Finland and Norway, alcohol was banned for some years in the early 1900s because of its affect on crime and violence.

▲ Beer is made by boiling and fermenting a mixture of malt and other ingredients.

Strengths Compared

DRINK	TYPE OF DRINK	PROOF (STRENGTH)
Alcopop	Soft drink and alcohol	4%-8%
Beer	Fermented grains and water	3%-10%
Liquers	Sweetened, flavoured spirits	20%-40%
Spirits	Alcohol concentrated by distillation	38%-45%
Wine	Fermented grape juice	8%-14%

Effect on the body

A little alcohol may make the drinker feel relaxed and carefree. But the more that is drunk, the worse they will feel. As more alcohol enters their blood, they will start to feel dizzy, lose their sense of balance and find it difficult to walk. They may start slurring their words and be sick.

▲ Too much alcohol can make everything seem to spin, which also causes nausea.

Alcohol in the Blood

When someone drinks alcohol, it is absorbed into their blood. In the blood, it travels to their brain and stops it working properly.

Dangers

Too much alcohol can kill. It causes alcohol poisoning, which damages the liver, and can make people collapse and fall asleep until their body gets rid of the poison. If a person is sick in their sleep, the vomit can choke and kill them. If alcohol is drunk very quickly, it can affect the brain so badly that the heart and breathing stops

People who drink too much can end up in hospital. ▼

Blood Alcohol Levels

The amount of alcohol in a person's blood is called their blood alcohol level. It is measured as milligrams (mg) per 100 millilitres (ml) of blood. The higher someone's blood alcohol level, the worse their symptoms. Here are some examples:

BLOOD ALCOHOL (mg/100ml)	EFFECT
20 mg	Feel relaxed.
100 mg	Unable to walk straight.
180 mg	Very drunk. May suffer memory loss later.
300 mg	May lose control of bladder and enter a coma.
500 mg	Likely to die without medical help.

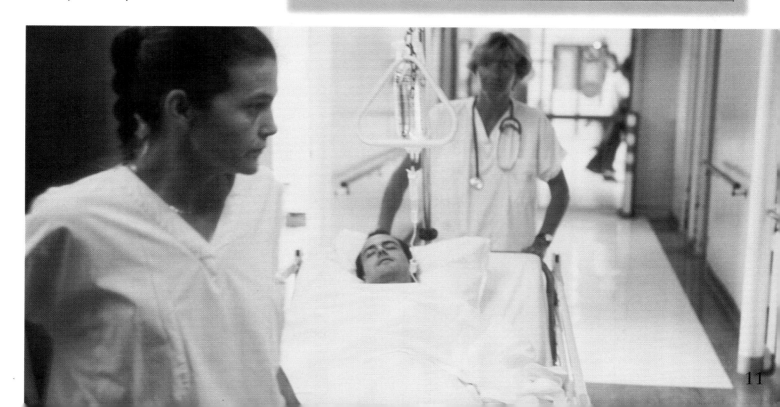

Affect on the mind

Alcohol affects the mind as well as the body. At first alcohol makes people feel happier and more confident. This is often the reason why people like to drink. But the more someone drinks, the worse they will feel. They may start to feel sad, their judgement will get worse and they may do things that they would not normally do. Many accidents, crimes and unwanted pregnancies happen when people get drunk.

Alcohol can make people feel happy at first. ▼

Units

Alcohol is measured in units. One unit of alcohol can be one small glass of wine, half a pint of medium-strength beer or a measure of spirits.

▲ Driving after drinking can cause fatal road accidents.

Memory loss

Alcohol can cause brain damage. People who get drunk can wake up the next morning and be unable to remember what they did the night before. They have permanently damaged their memory.

Drinking and Driving

Driving after drinking alcohol is extremely dangerous because alcohol affects a person's judgement. It also slows down the time it takes to react to hazards. Here are ways that alcohol affects driving according to blood alcohol level:

BLOOD ALCOHOL (mg/100ml)	AFFECT ON DRIVING
20-50 mg	Driver likely to take greater risks. Difficulty with judging speed.
50-79 mg	Slower reaction times so it takes longer to avoid hazards. Difficulty with judging distance.
over 80 mg	Poor vision and inability to see other cars or pedestrians.

13

Hangovers

Drinking too much can make people feel very ill the next day. This is called a hangover. Hangovers can include headaches, nausea, food cravings and poor sleep. These symptoms are all caused by the different ways that alcohol affects the body. Headaches are caused by alcohol dehydrating the body. Nausea is caused by alcohol upsetting the stomach. People get food cravings because alcohol lowers the levels of sugar in their blood. Poor sleep can be caused by the strain alcohol puts upon the liver.

◀ Vomiting is one method the body uses to get rid of alcoho poisoning.

Avoiding hangovers

Some people try to avoid hangovers by making sure they drink lots of water to avoid dehydration. Or they make sure they eat before they drink and don't mix different types of alcohol. But the only guaranteed way to avoid a hangover is not to drink.

Liver Damage

The liver is an organ in the body that helps digestion. It gets rid of poisons like alcohol. When there is too much alcohol for it to cope with, the liver is damaged.

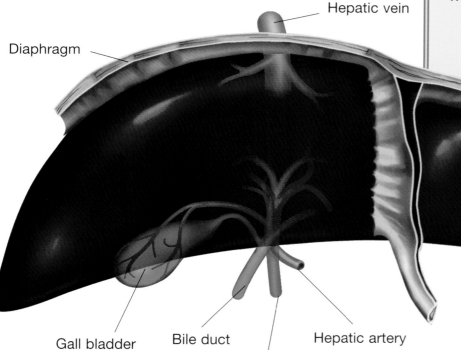

Hepatic vein

Diaphragm

Gall bladder

Bile duct

Portal vein

Hepatic artery

▲ This cross-section of a liver shows the paths of blood and waste products. Blood enters the liver through the portal vein and hepatic artery. It leaves through the hepatic vein after being processed. Waste products like alcohol leave through the bile duct.

DID YOU KNOW?

Every year in the UK, alcohol costs:

- about £2 billion for people being off work
- about £3 billion for absence from work, unemployment, premature deaths, and alcohol-related crime and accidents
- about £3 billion for hospital services

15

Long-term damage

Drinking too much over a long period of time can cause serious diseases. The liver can become so strained that it becomes scarred and stops working properly. This is called cirrhosis. Drinking can also lead to liver cancer and a disease called hepatitis, which makes the liver swollen. Heavy drinking can help bring about heart disease and stomach ulcers. It can make men sexually impotent and increases the risk of breast cancer in women. Women who drink while pregnant can seriously damage the child in their womb.

The scarred liver of someone with cirrhosis, a disease often caused by heavy drinking. ▼

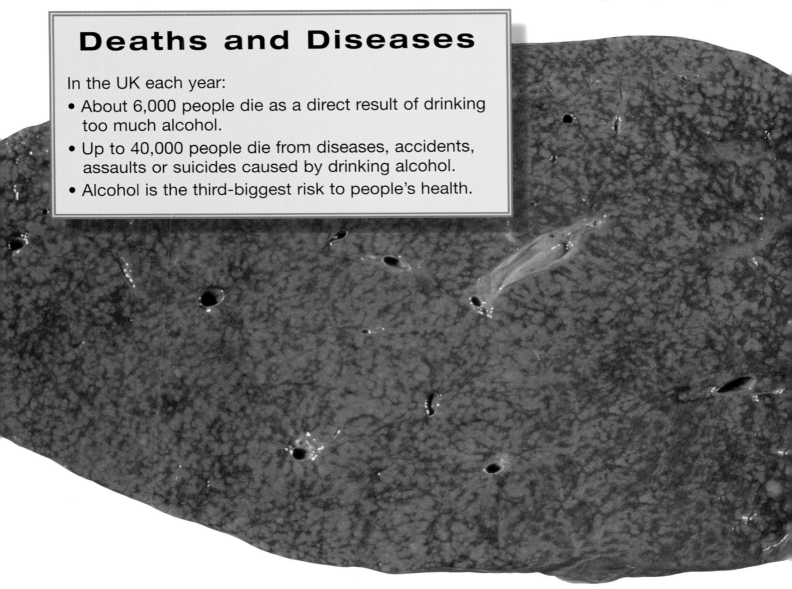

Deaths and Diseases

In the UK each year:
- About 6,000 people die as a direct result of drinking too much alcohol.
- Up to 40,000 people die from diseases, accidents, assaults or suicides caused by drinking alcohol.
- Alcohol is the third-biggest risk to people's health.

▲ A few glasses of wine can have as many calories as a whole meal.

Weight gain

Alcohol is very fattening. A pint of beer contains as many calories as a chocolate bar, so drinking can make you fat. But alcohol doesn't contain any vitamins or minerals, so people who drink instead of eat can become malnourished.

Women and Alcohol

Alcohol has a more serious effect on women than on men because they are generally smaller. This means the alcohol is more concentrated in their blood and has a stronger effect on their brains.

▲ Hangovers are a reminder of the damage alcohol does to your body.

Alcoholism

Heavy drinkers can become addicted to alcohol. They are known as alcoholics. No-one is certain why a person becomes an alcoholic. It may be in their genes, since alcoholism sometimes runs in families. Or it may be due to psychological problems, which make them drink to make their life more bearable. Alcoholics may lose their jobs if they find it difficult to work and their relationships with family and friends often suffer. These problems sometimes make them drink even more.

Alcoholism usually takes years to develop. At first, people just want to drink more of the time until they start drinking first thing in the morning. Whenever they drink, alcoholics usually get drunk. They may suffer from shaking, body pains and a red face. After they stop drinking, alcoholics can suffer from serious withdrawal symptoms, including confusion, hallucinations, violent trembling and sometimes death.

Treatment

Alcoholics can be successfully treated. Clinics can help them give up alcohol and cope with their withdrawal symptoms. Afterwards, groups like Alcoholics Anonymous (AA) can help their emotional problems and stop them drinking again.

Alcohol becomes the most important thing in an alcoholic's life and can destroy their relationships with family and friends. ▼

Smoking

Cigarettes are made using the dried leaves of the tobacco plant, which originally came from Central America. But there are thousands of other substances added to the tobacco. Some of these are used to make each brand of cigarette taste different.

The USA is the world's second-largest producer of tobacco.▼

Chemicals

Cigarettes contain thousands of chemicals that can cause lung cancer, heart disease, and other illnesses. The chemicals are in the form of either gases or tiny particles, called tar. One of the most dangerous chemicals is nicotine, which is a powerful addictive drug. The most hazardous gas is carbon monoxide, which is the same poisonous gas that comes out of car exhausts.

Cost

In 2004 in Britain, the average packet of cigarettes cost £4.75. For someone smoking a packet a day for 30 years, it would cost them over £50,000. For the same money, they could buy a flat or even a small house in some areas.

Cigarette machines can make about 4,000 cigarettes a minute. ▶

Affect on the body

When a person smokes, nicotine travels to the brain. It raises the heart rate and increases the blood pressure. It also suppresses the appetite and lowers the skin temperature.

At the same time, carbon monoxide gas combines with haemoglobin in the blood. Haemoglobin usually carries oxygen around the body.

◄ When someone gets a craving for a cigarette, they are feeling the effect of the drug nicotine acting upon their brain.

Pregnancy

If a pregnant woman smokes, less oxygen gets to her womb so her baby won't grow as fast. Babies born to smokers are more likely to be smaller, born prematurely, or to die just before or after birth.

Smoking can seriously damage an unborn baby's health by reducing the amount of oxygen they receive. ▶

Carbon monoxide

When carbon monoxide from cigarette smoke enters the blood, it reduces the amount of oxygen getting to tissues and body cells. The tissues need oxygen to function properly. If the body continues to be starved of oxygen, the tissues can have problems with growth and repair, which can lead to diseases like cancer.

Heart disease

When people smoke, the carbon monoxide they breathe in encourages fatty deposits in the heart's arteries. These deposits increase the risk of heart disease, which can lead to heart attacks. The heart is also put under stress by nicotine, which raises the heart rate and blood pressure. This also increases the risk of heart attacks.

These are just some of the diseases that may be caused by smoking. ▼

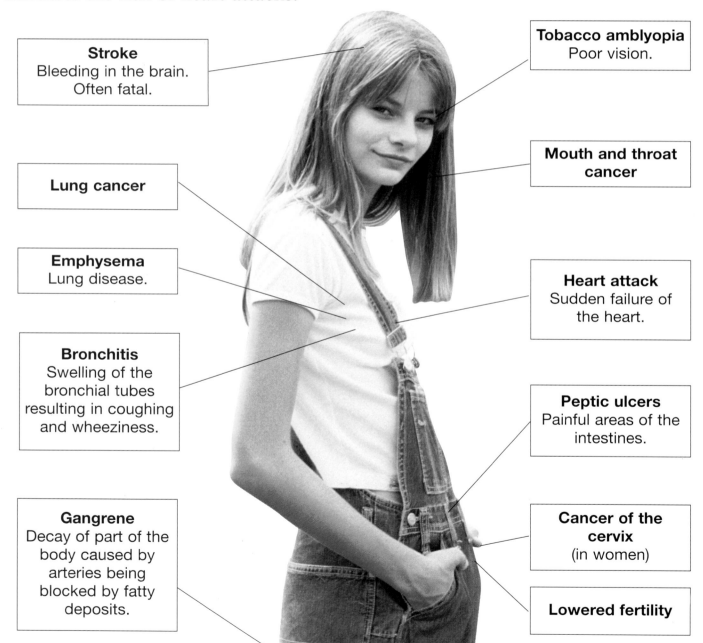

Stroke
Bleeding in the brain. Often fatal.

Lung cancer

Emphysema
Lung disease.

Bronchitis
Swelling of the bronchial tubes resulting in coughing and wheeziness.

Gangrene
Decay of part of the body caused by arteries being blocked by fatty deposits.

Tobacco amblyopia
Poor vision.

Mouth and throat cancer

Heart attack
Sudden failure of the heart.

Peptic ulcers
Painful areas of the intestines.

Cancer of the cervix
(in women)

Lowered fertility

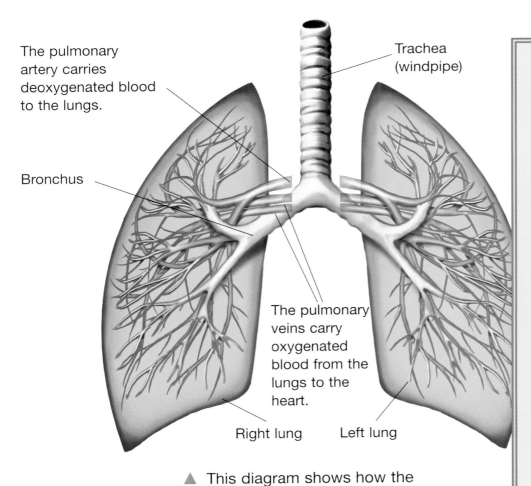

The pulmonary artery carries deoxygenated blood to the lungs.

Trachea (windpipe)

Bronchus

The pulmonary veins carry oxygenated blood from the lungs to the heart.

Right lung

Left lung

▲ This diagram shows how the lungs work. The lungs pass oxygen to the blood when we breathe in and release carbon dioxide gas when we breathe out.

Passive Smoking

Breathing in other people's cigarette smoke can kill. For babies and young children, it can cause pneumonia and other chest infections. For people who are exposed to other smokers over long periods of time, they are more likely to die from lung cancer by 10–30 per cent.

This smoker's lung is blackened, scarred and out of shape. ▼

Tar

Tar is another killer in cigarettes. Tiny chemical particles are inhaled through cigarette smoke and deposited in the lungs. The lungs become scarred and clogged up, leading to coughing and breathlessness. Unable to get rid of pollutants properly, smokers are more likely to suffer from bronchitis and other lung infections. They may develop a fatal lung disease, called emphysema. Many chemicals in tar can also cause lung cancer.

▲ It can be difficult for people to tell a friend that their cigarettes are irritating them.

Why people smoke

Many people start smoking in their teens. They may feel pressurised by their friends and want to feel part of 'the gang', or they may think it makes them look older or 'cool'. But just a few cigarettes·can quickly make them addicted. This is mainly due to nicotine, which produces withdrawal symptoms including cravings, tenseness and tiredness.

Smoking temporarily eases these symptoms before leaving smokers tense, tired and craving a cigarette again. The more cigarettes that are smoked, the greater the withdrawal symptoms. This can lead to chain-smoking, where smokers light a new cigarette immediately after putting one out. Chain-smokers can smoke up to 60 cigarettes a day.

Death rates

Every year in the UK, 120,000 people die from diseases related to smoking. Millions more suffer from coughing and bad breath caused by cigarettes.

Psychological addiction

If people get in the habit of having a cigarette after every meal, with a coffee or other occasion, they become psychologically addicted. It can be just as hard to give up these habits as coping with the physical cravings.

DID YOU KNOW?

In the UK:
- About 450 children under 16 years old start smoking every day.
- Over 1 billion cigarettes are smoked by children aged between 11 and 15 years old every year.
- Almost a quarter of 15-year-olds are regular smokers.

▲ People have a 90 per cent chance of becoming addicted to just a few cigarettes.

Giving up

Like all addictions, giving up isn't easy. Seven out of every ten smokers who try to give up fail at least twice. Many people manage to give up for years but take up smoking again in a stressful situation. The first few days are usually the hardest. This is when nicotine produces the worst withdrawal symptoms, such as light-headedness, anxiety, coughing and strong cravings. It takes a lot of willpower to overcome these physical symptoms.

Nicotine is as addictive as heroin, so the cravings to smoke are hard to resist. ▶

Help with giving up

Many smokers find they need more than just willpower to help them give up. Nicotine patches and gum can help by gradually reducing the nicotine in a person's body. Or hypnotism can be used to get rid of the urge to smoke.

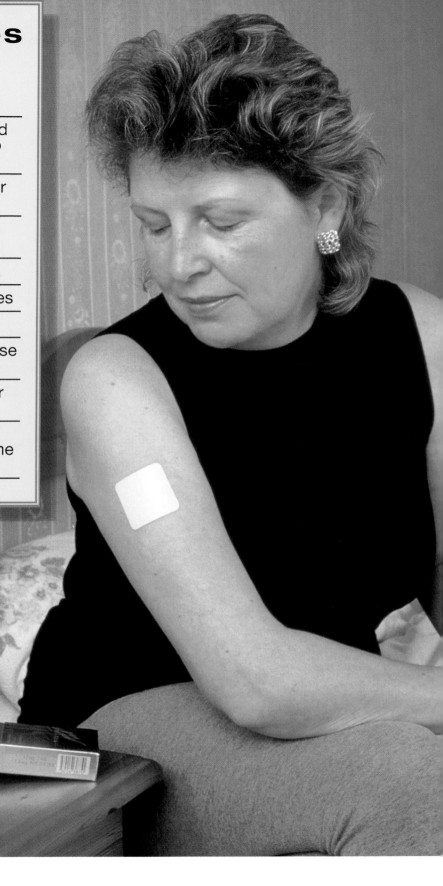

Recovery Stages

TIME AFTER LAST CIGARETTE	EFFECT ON BODY
20 minutes	Blood pressure and heart rate return to normal.
1 day	Lungs start to clear mucus.
2 days	Body is clear of nicotine.
3 days	Breathing is easier.
2–12 weeks	Circulation improves
3–9 months	Lungs work better.
1 year	Risk of heart disease is halved
10 years	Risk of lung cancer is halved.
15 years	Risk of death from smoking is the same as a non-smoker.

Many people have to change their routines at first and avoid situations where they would normally smoke. Within several months though, the urge to smoke disappears.

Nicotine patches reduce the urge to smoke by passing a small amount of nicotine through the skin. ▶

Illegal Drugs

People take illegal drugs for different reasons: for fun, because their friends are taking them, or to try and escape from their problems. But taking illegal drugs is a gamble because you can never be sure what is in them or how they will affect you.

Drugs act in different ways. Cocaine, ecstasy and speed are stimulants that increase the activity of the brain. Alcohol and solvents are depressants that slow down the brain's activity. Cannabis and LSD are hallucinogens that distort the way you see and hear things.

Types of Illegal Drugs

DRUG	STREET NAMES	USUAL FORM	HOW TAKEN
Amphetamine	Speed, whizz, uppers	Powder or tablets	Swallowed, sniffed, injected, smoked
Cannabis	Blow, dope, ganja, puff, weed	Brown/black resin or grass	Smoked or eaten
Cocaine	Charlie, snow, crack	White powder, crystals	Sniffed or smoked
Ecstasy	E, pills, doves	Pills	Swallowed
Heroin	Smack, horse, skag	Brown or white powder	Injected, sniffed or smoked
LSD	Acid, trips	Tablets, impregnated paper	Swallowed
Magic mushrooms	Shrooms, mushies	Dried/fresh mushrooms	Eaten
Sedatives	Barbiturates, Temazepam	Tablets	Swallowed
Solvents		Glue, lighter fuel, nail varnish, petrol, aerosol	Inhaled

Signs

It is not always obvious that someone has taken drugs. People who have taken cannabis or heroin may seem more quiet than usual. If they have taken amphetamines, cocaine or ecstasy they may seem more lively.

◀ You can never guarantee that an illegal drug won't make you feel terrible.

The effect of a drug depends on a person's size, what else is taken with it (such as alcohol) and how it is taken. Injecting or snorting a drug has a faster and more powerful effect than swallowing.

Left to right: Heroin, ecstasy, cannabis (grass)

Magic mushroom, LSD, cannabis resin

Cocaine, crack, speed

31

Effect on the mind

Different drugs have different ways of making people feel. Ecstasy can produce feelings of friendliness and happiness. Cannabis can make things seem funnier, or produce feelings of calm. But all illegal drugs can make you feel terrible. Cannabis can produce feelings of fear and paranoia. LSD and mushrooms can produce extreme feelings of anxiety, paranoia and nightmare hallucinations, known as 'bad trips'.

Drug Use

In the UK, about a quarter of all 16–29-year-olds take illegal drugs every year. About a third of the whole population have taken drugs at some point in their lives.

 When someone becomes paranoid, they start to distrust their friends and other people.

You can never be sure how you will react to an illegal substance. You might have taken it many times before and then suddenly have a bad reaction. It often depends on your mood. Cannabis will heighten whatever mood you are in when you take it, so if you are feeling sad, it will make you feel even worse.

Drugs and Their Effects

DRUG	GOOD FEELINGS	BAD FEELINGS	HOW LONG IT LASTS
Amphetamines	Wakefulness	Anxiety, insomnia	3–4 hours
Cannabis	Relaxation	Paranoia, panic	1–12 hours
Cocaine	Exhilaration	Insomnia, depression after use	20–30 minutes Crack lasts 10–12 minutes
Ecstasy	Happiness, friendliness	Nausea, depression after use	Several hours
Heroin	Happiness, peacefulness	Nausea, vomiting	3–4 hours
LSD/ Magic mushrooms	Euphoria, fascinating hallucinations	Nightmares, hallucinations paranoia	12 hours
Sedatives	Calmness, relaxation	Nausea, vomiting	Several hours
Solvents (glue)	Hallucinations, euphoria	Hangovers, drowsiness	A few minutes

Taking ecstasy in nightclubs is a dangerous trend because it is easy to get dehydrated and collapse. ▼

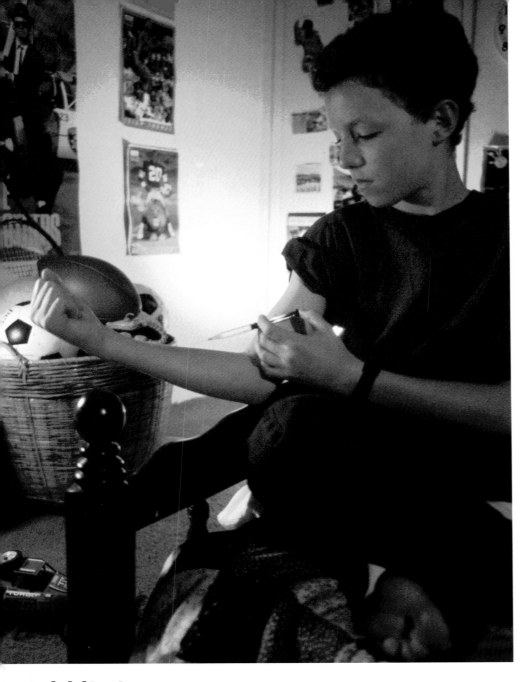

◀ This boy is using a syringe to inject himself with drugs. Parents may not realise their child is taking drugs until it is too late and he or she has become physically addicted.

Treatment

• People often need help to stop taking drugs. Methadone can help heroin addicts by easing their withdrawal symptoms.

• Rehabilitation clinics can help addicts give up in a supportive environment.

• Counselling can help psychological addicts work out why they feel they need a drug to enjoy themselves.

Addiction

It is easy to become addicted to drugs. This addiction can be psychological, physical, or a mixture of both. Cannabis, ecstasy, amphetamines, LSD and solvents are not physically addictive drugs. But if a person feels they cannot enjoy themselves without taking one of these drugs, they are psychologically addicted to it.

Heroin, cocaine, crack and sedatives are mainly physically addictive. If a person stops taking them, they suffer terrible physical withdrawal symptoms that can be quickly relieved by taking more. How quickly they become addicted depends on the drug, how much is taken, the personality of the user and other circumstances. Heroin may not be instantly addictive, but using crack cocaine just one time can make you instantly dependent.

Heroin and Crack

In the UK:

- Less than 1 per cent of the population use heroin.

- In 2000, 926 people died from using heroin.

- In 2000, 238 people died from using methadone.

- In 2001, 258,000 people were using heroin

◄ These vials contain crack cocaine crystals. Crack is a highly addictive drug. Users heat the crystals and inhale the vapour that comes off them.

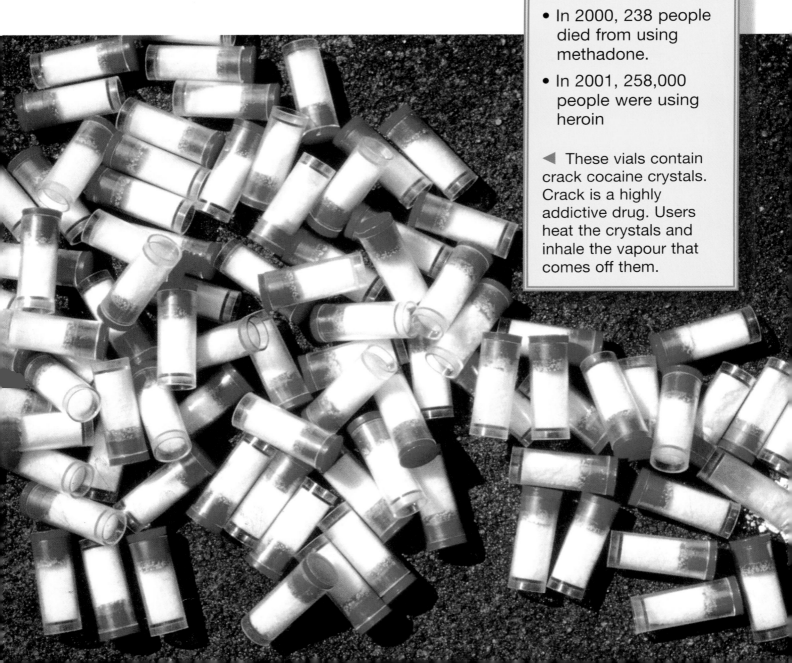

After the high

Drugs might make people feel good at first, but the effect soon wears off. Even drugs that are not physically addictive, like ecstasy, cause tiredness and depression afterwards. Some people call this 'coming down'. Many people find that the 'come down' isn't worth the high they get in first place.

▲ Addicts will commit crimes to get more drugs.

Drugs and Crime

- Drugs are very expensive, so many users have to steal to pay for their habit.
- Heroin and cocaine addicts need between £10,000 and £40,000 a year to pay for drugs.
- In the UK in 2001, 67% of the people arrested by the police and held in custody had taken drugs.
- In the UK, crime related to drugs costs over £2.5 billion a year.

Long-term damage

The immediate 'comedown' might feel bad, but the long-term damage of taking drugs can be far greater. Cocaine can cause heart problems and damage the lining of the nose. Ecstasy can cause liver and kidney problems. Amphetamines put a strain on the heart. Smoking cannabis can lead to throat and lung cancer.

Smoking cannabis over a long time can cause lack of motivation and difficulty in concentrating. If this affects a person's job, they may run into financial problems. Drug use over a long time can also change someone's personality and damage relationships with friends and family.

Mental Health

Some drugs can permanently damage mental health. Hallucinogens like LSD can lead to flashbacks, where people relive aspects of their 'trip' years afterwards. They can also bring on problems like depression and schizophrenia. Ecstasy can change the chemicals in the brain, leading to depression.

There has not been enough research on illegal drugs like amphetamine (below) so no one knows what the long-term effects may be. ▼

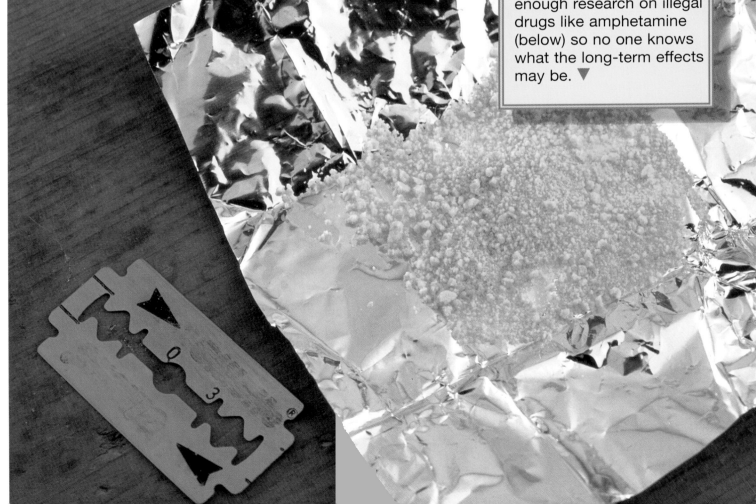

Drug deaths

Illegal drugs can kill. You can never tell exactly what is in them, who made them, or how you will react to those ingredients.

Drug Deaths

In 2000 in the UK:

- 3,495 people died from direct drug poisoning.
- 926 people died from taking heroine and morphine.
- 238 people died from taking methadone.
- 26 people died from taking ecstasy.

Heroin users cannot tell how concentrated the drug is before they inject it and heroin that is too 'pure' can be lethal. ▼

Killers

Combining different drugs, especially alcohol and illegal drugs, can cause a fatal reaction. Solvent abuse (glue-sniffing) can lead to suffocation, choking on vomit or heart failure. Heroin and crack cocaine can kill through overdose when the drug is more concentrated than expected. Ecstasy can kill by causing overheating and dehydration, yet some people have died from drinking too much water after taking ecstasy.

Not all deaths are directly caused by drugs but by the accidents they cause. Like alcohol, drugs alter a person's judgement and can make them do things they would not normally do. Each year thousands of traffic and other accidental deaths are caused by people under the influence of drugs.

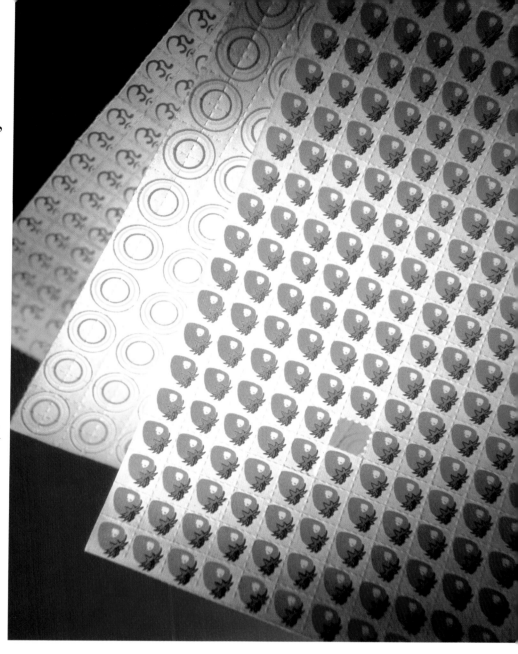

▲ LSD comes as tablets or as squares of blotting paper saturated with the drug.

Hallucinogenics

LSD and magic mushrooms cause hallucinations, where the mind sees and hears things that aren't really there. These can be lethal if the user is driving, on a balcony or simply walking along a pavement because they may forget where they are and do something foolish.

Medicinal Drugs

Drugs used as medicines save the lives of millions of people every year, and help us live longer and healthier than our ancestors ever did. Before the twentieth century, all medicinal drugs came from plants, and herbal medicines are still popular today. Echinacea comes from a plant and can be used to strengthen the immune system and St John's wort can help to treat depression.

Thousands of new drugs are developed each year but some illnesses, such as the common cold, still have no cure. ▶

Placebo Effect

When drugs are tested, one group of people is given the real drug while a pretend drug is given to a second group. Neither group know which has the real drug, but sometimes even people in the pretend group find that their symptoms improve. This is known as the placebo effect.

Antibiotics are used to treat diseases caused by bacteria. They can cure many diseases that were once fatal. ▶

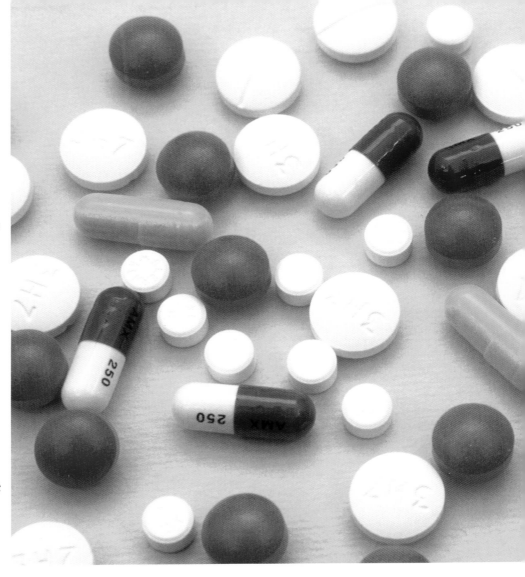

Modern drugs

Most modern drugs are now created in laboratories using various chemical processes. There are drugs for every type of illness, and thousands of new ones are developed by scientists every year. Most work on the body in one of the following ways:

1. Fight infection
2. Prevent infectious disease
3. Affect the heart and blood vessels, or
4. Affect the nervous system.

Side effects

Medicinal drugs work on the whole body, not just the area that is affected by the illness. This means that as well as the desired effects on the ill part of the body, there are additional effects, called side effects. Some people feel the side effects more than others.

Side Effects

DRUG	USE	SIDE EFFECTS
Prozac	Anti-depressant	Headaches, diarrhoea, anxiety
Aspirin	Painkilller	Indigestion
Morphine	Painkiller	Sleepiness, nausea, constipation
Antibiotics	Anti-infection drug	Diarrhoea, rash

Drugs for Sport

DRUG	WHY TAKEN	IS IT BANNED?	WHY?
Steroids	To build muscle.	Yes	Gives users an unfair advantage and can cause illness.
Caffeine	To stimulate the body	No	
Cocaine	To stimulate the body	Yes	Damages the health.
Morphine	To reduce pain	Yes	Can hide other problems.

Steroids build muscles, so they can improve a person's performance in a competition. ▼

Dangers

Even medicinal drugs can be dangerous if they are not used properly. All drugs are chemicals, which can poison the body if taken in too great a quantity. Some medicinal drugs are used for the wrong reasons. Temazepam is a sleeping pill that should only be prescribed by a doctor, but some people buy it illegally to make them feel good. If it is not taken properly, it can kill. Some drugs are taken by accident. Many children have died after mistaking aspirin for sweets.

Some people have a bad reaction to a medicinal drug that they need to fight disease. But if they don't take the medicine, they can die. Sometimes drugs react badly when mixed with another drug, like alcohol. Alcohol can also stop medicinal drugs working properly.

Medicinal drugs are dangerous for certain people. Aspirin can be very dangerous if taken accidentally by young children and many drugs are not suitable for pregnant women because they may damage the unborn child.

▲ When doctors advise a patient to take medicinal drugs, they write a prescription with instructions on how to take them.

Cancer

Chemotherapy is a treatment for cancer that poisons certain cells in the body on purpose. It only poisons cells affected by the cancer, so the healthy cells can recover. It can however, have some unpleasant side-effects such as hair loss and sickness.

Handle with Care

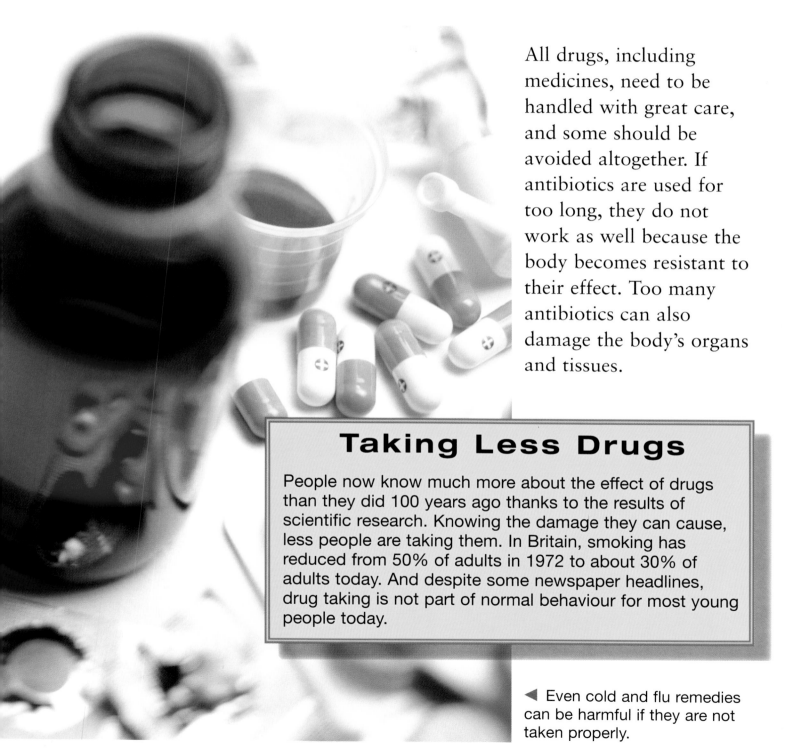

All drugs, including medicines, need to be handled with great care, and some should be avoided altogether. If antibiotics are used for too long, they do not work as well because the body becomes resistant to their effect. Too many antibiotics can also damage the body's organs and tissues.

Taking Less Drugs

People now know much more about the effect of drugs than they did 100 years ago thanks to the results of scientific research. Knowing the damage they can cause, less people are taking them. In Britain, smoking has reduced from 50% of adults in 1972 to about 30% of adults today. And despite some newspaper headlines, drug taking is not part of normal behaviour for most young people today.

◀ Even cold and flu remedies can be harmful if they are not taken properly.

Too much alcohol can cause both short-term illness (hangovers) and long-term damage to the body's organs. But alcohol doesn't have to be harmful if it is drunk in moderation, and small amounts of alcohol can actually be good for you.

However, if you care about your health and want to feel good throughout your life, you should avoid tobacco, cannabis and other illegal drugs. They damage your health even in small amounts and sometimes you won't know what that damage will be until years to come. By that time, it will be too late to do anything about it.

◀ Coffee, beer and wine are enjoyed by millions of people around the world without damaging their health.

45

Glossary

addictive The power of a substance that is difficult to give up.

alcoholic Someone who is addicted to drinking too much alcohol.

arteries Blood vessels that carry blood from the heart to the rest of the body.

blood alcohol The amount of alcohol in a person's blood, measured in milligrams per 100 millilitres of blood.

blood pressure The pressure of blood against the walls of the blood vessels.

calories Units of energy supplied by food.

cancer Any of several diseases where cells grow in harmful way.

carbon monoxide A poisonous gas produced when carbon burns in a small amount of air.

coma A state of unconsciousness caused by disease, injury or poison.

dehydration Lacking water.

depressants Drugs that relax the body's muscles and reduce its reactions.

distillation A process where a substance is made pure by turning it into a gas and then cooling it to form a liquid again.

emotional To do with the emotions, or feelings, rather than the body.

euphoria A strong feeling of happiness.

fermented A substance that has been changed by turning sugar into alcohol.

fertility The ability to produce young.

hallucinogens Drugs that cause hallucinations, where the mind sees and hears things that are not really there.

hangover A condition caused by drinking too much alcohol.

heart attack The sudden failure of the heart to keep pumping blood around the body.

herbal medicines Medicines from plants.

impotent Powerless.

malnourished A condition caused by eating the wrong types and not enough food, so the body lacks essential nutrients.

nausea Feeling sick.

nicotine A poisonous and addictive substance found in the tobacco plant.

oxygen A gas found in the air that we use to breathe and make energy.

paranoia A form of mental illness where someone feels that other people do not like them or they are being persecuted.

physical To do with the body rather than the mind.

psychological To do with the mind.

schizophrenia A form of mental illness where a person suffers from a split personality.

stimulant A substance that increases the activity of the body or part of the body.

Finding Out More

Books to read

Choices and Decisions series: *Drinking Alcohol, Smoking, Taking Drugs*, all by Steve Myers & Pete Saunders (Franklin Watts, 2004)
Get Wise: Drugs – What's the Danger? by Sarah Medina (Heinemann, 2004)
Health Issues series: *Alcohol, Amphetamines, Cannabis, Cocaine, Drugs, Heroin, Solvents,* by various authors (Hodder Wayland, 2003)
In the News: Drug Culture by Andrea Smith (Franklin Watts, 2003)
It Happened to Me: Drug Addict by Suzie Hayman (Franklin Watts, 2002)
Talking About: Drugs by Bruce Sanders (Franklin Watts, 2004)
What's at Issue?: Drugs and You by Bridget Lawless (Heinemann, 2000)
World Issues: Drugs by Jonathan Rees (Chrysalis, 2003)

Organizations

Health Education Authority
Trevelyan House,
30 Great Peter Street
London SW1P 2HW
Tel. 020 7413 1888

Alcohol Concern
Waterbridge House,
32-36 Loman Street
London SE1 OEE
Tel. 020 7928 7377

Alcoholics Anonymous
PO Box 1, Stonebow House
York YO1 2NJ
Tel: 01904 644026

Ash
16 Fitzhardinge Street
London W1H 9PL
Tel: 020 7224 0743

Institute for the Study of Drug Dependence
32-36 Loman Street
London SE1 OEE
Tel: 020 7928 1211

Index